Mastering People, Money, and Business

OrangeBooks Publication

1st Floor, Rajhans Arcade, Mall Road, Kohka, Bhilai, Chhattisgarh 490020
Website: **www.orangebooks.in**

First Edition, 2025

ISBN: 978-93-7426-870-4

Price: Rs. 249.00

Printed in India

MASTERING

PEOPLE, MONEY, AND BUSINESS

PREMRAJ BISHNOI

Orange Books Publication
www.orangebooks.in

Dedication

Dedicated to everyone who dreams of making life simple, not by luck, but by right decisions.

To the young dreamers, struggling workers, and silent thinkers who wish to understand people, money, and the mind.

May this book be your guide to live with clarity, confidence, and calm success.

Title: Mastering People, Money, and Business: My Journey from Village to Wakati Pharmacy.

Author: Premraj Bishnoi

Introduction

This book may teach you the same things which life teaches us every single day — sometimes with a smile, sometimes with a fall.

Some people forget those lessons, but a few turn them into a way of living.

This book is for those who want to understand life, people, and money — the real way.

My name is Premraj Bishnoi.

I was born in a small village in Jodhpur, Rajasthan — a place where even dreams were often kept small.

But I learned early that dreams have no limits — only our belief does.

This book brings together my experiences, lessons from my journey, and the wisdom I've gained from people, books, and real life.

It's not just a book about business or money — it's a book about understanding life itself.

It Explains —

- why people trust,
- how we make the right decisions,
- and how changing your thinking can change your world.

When I started Wakati Pharmacy, I realised something powerful — business doesn't run only on hard work.

It runs on understanding people, building a strong team, and making the right choices.

That's when I understood that leadership isn't about giving orders —

It's about giving direction, purpose, and belief.

What This Book Will Give You

Inside This Book, You Will Discover:

- The Power of Leadership Energy — how to awaken the energy that inspires others.

- The Psychology of Trust — why people believe, buy, and follow you.

- The Human Game — understanding the real behaviour behind faces and words.

- The Psychology of Money — how wealth begins in the mind before the bank.

- Building a Business People Love — where success means respect, not just revenue.

This book is for everyone who wants to make life easier—not through luck, but through the right decisions.

Every page carries a thought, every chapter a direction, and the whole book carries one message:

"Life becomes
easier when you
choose to live it
wisely."

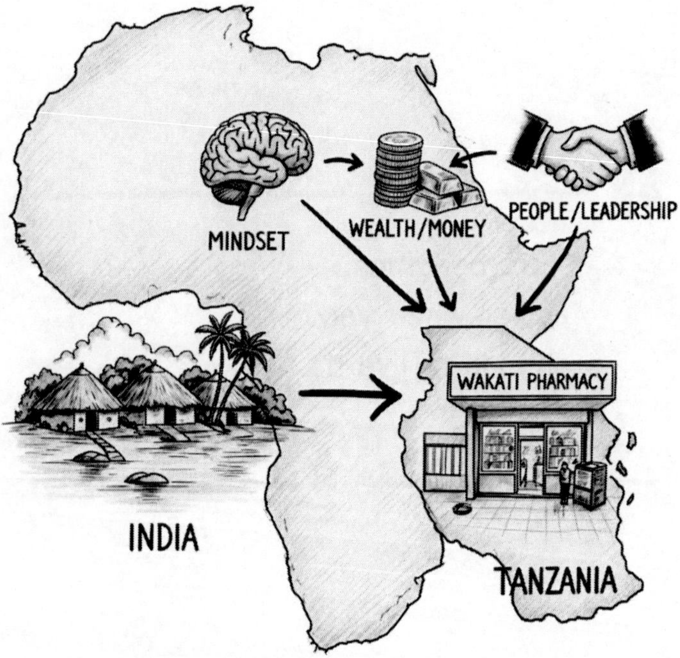
MINDSET
WEALTH/MONEY
PEOPLE/LEADERSHIP
WAKATI PHARMACY
INDIA
TANZANIA

Table of Contents

Chapter - 1

The Journey of Wakati – Time, Work, and the Human Mind

Every story has a beginning, but not every beginning looks like success.

Mine began in a small village outside **Jodhpur, Rajasthan**, where the desert wind carried both dust and dreams.

I was born on **10th January 1996**, into a simple family—three brothers, one sister, and parents who taught me values without ever using those words.

My father went to school only till the third grade. My mother never saw a classroom.

But together, they were the best teachers I could have had—one taught me *discipline*, the other *devotion.*

1. The Village Classroom

My first school was a government one.

I was never top of the class. In fact, I struggled badly in English and mathematics. But life had already started teaching me its own subjects — hard work, survival, and observation.

I saw my father work long hours under the sun, helping others build their houses while dreaming of improving our own. I watched him do small trades, helping people build and earn his way with dignity.

That was my first lesson in entrepreneurship — business starts not with money, but with courage.

When school holidays started, my father advised me to find a small job to earn for my college fees. So, I joined a small *kirana* (grocery) shop in Jodhpur.

I worked 14 hours a day carrying rice, sugar, and wheat bags — sweating, lifting, learning. I earned little, but gained a lot .

> **That one year shaped my mindset. It taught me: "If you can work hard when no one is watching, success will find you when everyone is."**

2. Learning Systems at Rishi Toyota

After finishing high school, I took a computer course — Tally, typing, and O-Level. It was the first technical skill I ever learned, and it gave me a way out of the village cycle.

In 2013, I joined **Rishi Toyota** for a monthly salary of ₹6,000 .

It was my first formal job, and I treated it like a temple of learning.

There, I discovered how *systems* make a business strong. I saw that a company doesn't just sell cars — it builds relationships, processes, and teamwork.

I Met Two People Who Shaped My Path:

- My manager — a disciplined leader who taught me how to think clearly under pressure.

- my colleague — a friend who later became the bridge to my destiny.

In Those Three Years, I Learned:

- How to manage conflicts
- How to work under pressure
- How to follow systems
- How to think like a leader, not just an employee

> **It was at Rishi Toyota that I realized: "Leadership is not a title — it's a way of thinking."**

3. The Leap to a New World

In 2016, Ravi Mathur called me in **Tanzania**.

He said, "There's a job opportunity here. It's tough, but you'll learn."

I had never left India before. The idea of moving to Africa sounded huge, even risky. But something inside me said, *"This is your time."*

That's how my journey in Tanzania began.

I started working at **Medox Pharmaceutical**.

This company taught me how to run a business — not from textbooks, but from the realities of people, market, and trust.

4. The Real MBA — Learning Business from the Ground Up

At Medox, I learned to:

- Talk to customers in a way that builds trust
- Study suppliers and understand negotiation
- Lead teams and motivate them beyond salary
- Manage money and understand profit, not just sales
- Handle pressure when things go wrong

I also learned something much deeper: **business is psychology in motion.**

People buy from people they trust.

Employees work hard for leaders they respect.

Suppliers cooperate with partners who are fair and consistent.

Every day was a lesson in human behaviour — the real subject no one teaches you in school.

5. Building Wakati Pharmacy

After eight years of learning, observing, and preparing, I decided to start something of my own — **Wakati Pharmacy Limited**.

We chose the name *Wakati*, meaning *time*, this name given by my business partner in Wakati Pharmacy. Wakati because everything I achieved in life happened at the right time — when I was ready for it.

Building Wakati Pharmacy was not just about selling medicine.

It Was About Building a Culture:

- A place where people feel proud to work
- A system where customers are respected
- A brand that represents honesty and care

I started facing real challenges — government approvals, licenses, delays, competition, financial pressure.

But every problem pushed me to become mentally stronger, more strategic, and emotionally stable.

> **I realized:**
> **"A businessman doesn't solve problems — he outgrows them."**

6. From Survival to Leadership

As Wakati Pharmacy grew, I started managing teams. That's when I understood the real meaning of leadership—it's not about controlling people; it's about inspiring them. You can't buy loyalty; you have to *earn* it.

I learned to listen more than I talk.

To study people's behaviour, not just their words.

To appreciate effort, not just results.

The company became a mirror of my mindset.

The stronger I became mentally, the stronger Wakati grew.

7. The Awakening

After years of reading books on psychology, money, and leadership — from authors like Napoleon Hill, Robert Greene, Morgan Housel, and Dale Carnegie — I realised all those lessons were already hidden in my own story.

I had lived with them.

I had seen how mindset changes destiny.

How emotions drive financial decisions.

How can people be led through trust, not fear?

That realisation planted the seed for this book. Because I wanted to share with others what life had already taught me — that **human psychology, emotional intelligence, and time** are the real currencies of success.

Closing Thought

From a village boy carrying rice bags to running a growing pharmacy on another continent—the journey taught me one thing above all

> "Time doesn't just pass — it tests you. And if you learn from those tests, time rewards you."
>
> That's what Wakati means to me.

Chapter - 2

The Mind Before the Money

Most people think success starts with money. They're wrong. It starts with how you think.

You can give two people the same opportunity, same market, same amount of money — one will grow it, the other will lose it.

The difference is not luck. It's the mindset.

When I started working in business, I thought the smartest person wins. Later, I learned it's not about who knows more — it's about who understands people better.

Because business is not just about products or numbers; it's about psychology — how humans think, act, and make decisions.

1. The Hidden Engine of Every Decision

Every choice we make — what to buy, who to trust, when to take a risk — comes from invisible emotions we rarely admit. *fear, desire, ego, and validation.*

- **Fear** stops people from taking action.
- **Desire** makes people chase shortcuts.
- **Ego** blinds people from learning.
- **Validation** makes people do things only to be seen.

If you can understand these four forces — in yourself and in others — you will start seeing through the surface of human behaviour. And once you see that clearly, you can predict people. And when you can predict people, you can *lead them.*

2. The Psychology of Scarcity

Most people are trained to think like survivors, not creators.

They focus on what they *lack*, not what they *can build.*

That's why even when they earn more, they still feel poor.

Money doesn't change the mindset — it only *amplifies* it. A fearful person becomes a fearful investor. A greedy person becomes a careless spender. A confident person builds wealth steadily.

The goal is not just to earn more money — it's to *upgrade the software of your mind* that runs your financial life.

3. Business Is Human Behaviour in Action

Every business is a reflection of the people behind it. A business built by people who only chase money will eventually fall apart. A business built by people who understand trust, timing, and teamwork will grow even when the market falls.

If you study any great leader — from a local entrepreneur to a global CEO — they all have one thing in common:

They understand why people do what they do.

That's psychology.

That's leadership.

That's business.

4. The First Rule of Mastery

Before you lead others, you must lead yourself.

Before you manage people, you must manage your emotions.

Before you control money, you must control your mind.

The most powerful investment is not in stocks or property—it's in *mental clarity.*

Because once your thinking becomes clear, your decisions follow the same path — calm, confident, and consistent.

5. A Reflection for You

Take a few minutes and ask yourself:

- Do I make decisions from fear or from confidence?

- Do I want money to feel secure or to feel superior?
- Do I truly listen when people talk, or do I only wait to respond?
- Am I reacting, or am I leading?

Your answers to these questions will tell you where your journey of leadership and wealth truly begins.

Quote to Close the Chapter

"The real power is not having more money — it's having the mind that knows how to create it again and again."

Chapter - 3

The Psychology of Trust – Why People Buy, Follow, and Believe

In business, you don't sell products — you sell *trust.*

In leadership, you don't command people — you earn *belief.*

And in life, you don't attract respect — you *build* it, one honest action at a time.

When I started Wakati Pharmacy, I didn't have a big marketing team or millions in investment. What I had was an **understanding of people** — how they think, how they feel, and what makes them believe.

I learned that no matter where you are in the world — a customer in Dodoma, an employee in your team, or a supplier abroad — all human beings are built from the same raw material: *emotion.*

People don't buy medicine.

They buy *trust* in the person who sells it.

1. The Invisible Currency

Money is the visible transaction; trust is the invisible one.

Every successful business is built on that invisible exchange.

When a customer walks into your store, they are asking themselves silently:

- Can I trust this person with my money?
- Will they give me the right product, or just what gives them profit?
- Do they care about me, or just my wallet?

The answers to those questions decide the sale, not your price list.

Over the years, I've seen this again and again:

"If you win a customer's trust once, they will forgive your mistakes.

But if you break their trust once, even perfection won't bring them back."

That's why every employee at Wakati Pharmacy is taught one rule before anything else:

"Don't sell for today — build for tomorrow."

2. How Trust Is Formed

Psychology tells us that trust is formed through three invisible signals:

1. **Competence** — You know what you're doing.

2. **Consistency** — You keep your word again and again.

3. **Care** — You genuinely want the other person to do well.

You can't fake any of these for long. Customers and employees may not understand your business numbers—but they always sense your intentions.

If you tell a customer, "I don't have that medicine now, but I can bring it for you tomorrow," and then when you actually do, they'll remember that feeling of reliability longer than any sort of discount you offer.

Trust, once built, becomes your biggest marketing asset. It spreads silently — customer to customer, supplier to supplier, one honest word at a time.

3. The Trust Equation

Here's a truth I discovered in my years of business:

Trust = Truth × Time

The more truth you practice, and the longer you stay consistent with it, the stronger your trust becomes.

But if you lie once, that equation collapses — because time cannot multiply falsehood.

That's why short-term tricks never lead to long-term success.

Many businesses fail not because they lacked opportunity, but because they wanted to grow faster than trust could carry them.

4. Inside the Mind of the Follower

Leadership is another side of the same coin.

Employees don't follow you because of your title — they follow how you *make them feel.*

At Wakati Pharmacy, I realised that people work harder not for money alone, but for **recognition, belonging, and respect.**

If you listen to their ideas, appreciate their effort, and stand beside them in tough days, they start believing in your mission as their own.

A true leader creates emotional safety.

When people feel safe, they open up, they share, and they innovate.

That's the psychology of loyalty — it's emotional, not transactional.

5. The Power of Listening

Trust is not built by talking more. It's built by *listening deeply.*

I've seen customers who walk into the store frustrated because of a bad experience elsewhere — but when you let them speak, understand their pain, and respond calmly, they leave not just satisfied, but connected.

In human psychology, listening is one of the most powerful forms of respect. It silently tells the other person:

"You matter."

That feeling builds relationships stronger than any sales pitch ever could.

6. When Trust Is Tested

Every business faces a point when things go wrong — a delayed delivery, a supplier issue, a misunderstanding. That's when your true brand is revealed.

When you admit a mistake openly and fix it fast, people trust you more — not less.

Because they see *humanness*, not perfection.

The greatest companies in the world are not those that never fail; they are the ones that never hide when they do.

7. Lessons from Wakati Pharmacy

From my years building Wakati, I've learned a few unshakable truths about trust:

1. **Be honest when it's hard.** That's when it counts.

2. **Never promise what you can't deliver.** Short-term lies are long-term poison.

3. **Treat everyone with respect — customers, staff, or suppliers.** The way you treat people who can't give you anything shows your real character.

4. **Train your team to think long-term.** Sales last a day; trust lasts a lifetime.

5. **Keep your word.** Every time you do, your reputation compounds like interest.

These are not theories; they are the real psychology that built my company from nothing.

8. The Circle of Belief

When customers trust you, they buy from you.

When employees trust you, they build with you.

When suppliers trust you, they grow with you.

And when all three believe in you, you no longer run a business.

You lead a movement.

That is the true power of trust — it multiplies through people faster than money ever can.

Closing Reflection

If you want to grow in business or leadership, start here:

Earn trust before profit.

Because profit is a result, but trust is a foundation.
And only foundations survive storms.

> "People don't follow what you say. They follow what they feel when they are around you."

That's the psychology of trust — invisible, but undeniable.

Chapter - 4

Leadership Energy – How to Move People Without Force

Leadership is not about power.

It's about **energy** — the kind that moves people when you walk into a room, speak a word, or make a decision.

Anyone can give orders. But true leaders don't push; they *pull.*

They attract effort, loyalty, and respect — not through fear, but through *presence.*

I learned this truth not from books, but from real life — from running Wakati Pharmacy, from managing people with different mindsets , emotions, and expectations.

In business, leadership is tested every single day — in silence, under pressure, and in how you handle people when things go wrong.

1. Leadership Is an Energy Field

Every leader carries an energy that people can feel even before they speak.

It's Made Of:

- **Confidence** (the courage to decide)
- **Calmness** (the ability to stay centred under pressure)

- **Clarity** (the vision that others can trust)

You don't need to shout to lead — your *energy* does the talking.

People subconsciously read your tone, eyes, and body language.

If your energy says, "We can do it," they believe it.

If your energy says "I'm unsure," they hesitate.

That's why I always tell my team:

"Before you manage others, manage your own energy."

2. The Psychology of Influence

Influence begins with understanding what drives people.

Some are motivated by recognition.

Some by purpose.

Some by progress.

Few by money alone.

Once you know what drives your team, you stop pushing and start *guiding*.

At Wakati, I learned to observe quietly: how people react, when they lose focus, what makes them excited.

The moment you understand their inner world; you unlock their best performance.

That's leadership psychology — *less control, more connection.*

3. Respect Over Fear

A leader has two ways to gain obedience: fear or respect.

Fear makes people work when you watch them.

Respect makes them work even when you're not there.

I've seen both kinds of leaders — those who shout and those who inspire.

The ones who inspire always win in the long run.

Because fear burns energy, respect builds it.

At Wakati Pharmacy, I learned to treat everyone — from the delivery person to the tech pharmacist — with the same tone of respect.

That consistency builds invisible trust, and trust turns into performance.

4. Emotional Stability: The Silent Power

Leadership energy is not loud; it's *steady.*

When things go wrong — a delayed shipment, an angry customer, or a bad sales week — your reaction sets the emotional temperature of the whole team.

If you panic, everyone panics.

If you stay calm, everyone steadies.

That's why leadership starts with emotional discipline.

A stable mind is like a lighthouse — when the sea is rough, everyone looks toward it for direction.

"Strong leaders are not those who never feel pressure.

They are those who remain centred while feeling it."

5. Communication That Moves People

The most powerful communication doesn't come from words — it comes from *tone, intent, and truth.*

People follow leaders who speak from the heart and logic at the same time.

At Wakati, when I call a meeting, I don't talk about tasks first — I talk about *purpose*.

Why we're doing, what we're doing.

How each role matters.

That "why" lights up people's inner motivation more than any salary can.

Good Communication in Leadership Means:

- Speak less, mean more
- Listen deeply
- Appreciate publicly, correct privately
- Replace blame with responsibility

These small habits turn words into movement.

6. The Energy of Example

The highest form of leadership is **example.**

You can't ask people to be disciplined if you're not.

You can't preach honesty if you manipulate things.

You can't expect teamwork if your ego leads.

People don't follow your instructions; they mirror your behaviour.

Every day, your actions broadcast your values louder than any speech.

That's why I always remind myself:

"You can't transfer energy you don't have."

When you stay consistent, passionate, and fair, people start reflecting your energy naturally. That's how a culture is born.

7. Turning Pressure into Purpose

There's a moment every leader faces — when things fall apart, when everyone looks at you for answers and you have none.

In those moments, leadership energy means **turning fear into focus.**

Instead of saying "We have a problem," I've learned to say, "We have a challenge — and a chance to grow."

The words may sound small, but they rewire everyone's mindset instantly.

Because people don't rise from commands — they rise from *confidence.*

8. Leadership Is a Mirror

Your business reflects your inner world.

If you're confused, your team will be too.

If you're confident, your team will act strongly.

If you're negative, your business will carry that energy in every corner.

That's why leadership is first an *inner game.*

Once your thoughts are clear and your emotions stable, your external results start aligning naturally.

9. Lessons That Built My Leadership Energy

From all the years of running Wakati Pharmacy, here are truths I'll never forget:

1. **Stay calm in chaos.** It earns silent respect.
2. **Listen before judging.** People open up when they feel heard.
3. **Give recognition often.** It multiplies motivation.
4. **Never lead with ego.** Ego blinds, empathy connects.
5. **Make people feel important**. That's how loyalty grows.

10. Closing Reflection

Leadership energy is not something you force — it's something you *become.*

It's built through experience, reflection, and emotional maturity.

When your intentions are clean, your vision clear, and your actions consistent, people feel your energy even in silence.

They don't just follow you; they believe in you.

That's the kind of leader I strive to be every day — not the one who controls, but the one who *creates movement.*

"A real leader doesn't push people to move.

He lights a fire inside them — and they move on their own."

Chapter - 5

The Human Game – How Emotions Control Every Decision

Every human you meet is playing a game — not against you, but within themselves.

The game is invisible, emotional, and deeply psychological.

It decides who wins in business, who leads in life, and who keeps repeating the same mistakes.

We all like to believe we are rational creatures.

But the truth? We are emotional first, logical second.

Every decision — to buy, to love, to quit, to trust — is made in the emotional brain first and later justified by logic.

Once you understand this game, you stop being surprised by people's behaviour.

You start to read it, lead it, and use it wisely.

1. The Illusion of Logic

Ask someone why they bought a product, and they'll say, "It had good quality."

Ask why they left a job, and they'll say, "Better opportunity."

Ask why they fell in love, and they'll say, "It just felt right."

That's the keyword — *felt.*

Behind every logical reason lies an emotional cause.

Logic is just the story we tell ourselves afterwards.

In sales, leadership, or relationships, people act on *feeling*—safety, pride, excitement, belonging, fear, or trust.

If you touch their emotions, you win their decision.

If you miss it, logic won't save you.

2. Emotions Are the Steering Wheel of Life

Imagine life as a car.

Logic is the map — but emotion is the steering wheel.

You can have the best plan, but if fear grabs the wheel, you'll stop.

If greed grabs it, you'll crash.

If confidence holds, you'll move fast and smart.

Most people think they control their emotions.

But in reality, their emotions control them — quietly, every day.

A leader, a salesperson, or an investor who can master emotion holds the real power — not over others, but over themselves.

3. The Hidden Drivers of Behaviour

There are five emotions that control most human decisions:

1. **Fear** — of loss, rejection, or failure
2. **Desire** — for success, recognition, love, or comfort
3. **Pride** — the need to protect self-image
4. **Belonging** — the wish to be accepted or part of something
5. **Hope** — the belief that tomorrow can be better

When you understand which one is driving a person at that moment, you can predict their behaviour almost perfectly.

At Wakati Pharmacy, I learned this while dealing with customers and staff.

A customer buying medicine is not just buying pills — they're buying *hope* for health.

A team member asking for a raise may not want money alone — they want *recognition.*

Every action hides an emotion.

Once you learn to see it, communication becomes easy.

4. Emotional Currency in Business

Money moves through emotion.

Every transaction is emotional energy exchanged for physical value.

Think About It:

People spend on what makes them *feel* better — safer, smarter, more respected, more beautiful.

That's why marketing that speaks to emotions always wins over one that speaks to features.

When I design a business pitch, I focus less on "what we sell" and more on "how people will feel after buying."

Because emotion is the *real currency* of human decision-making.

5. Emotional Intelligence — The Real Superpower

In school, we learn math, language, and science.

But the one subject that decides success in life — *emotional intelligence (EQ)* — is rarely taught.

EQ Means the Ability To:

- Understand your own emotions
- Manage them under pressure
- Read emotions in others
- Respond wisely instead of reacting blindly

In leadership, high EQ means your team feels safe around you.

In business, it means customers trust you.

In life, it means you stay peaceful even when chaos surrounds you.

Emotional intelligence turns life from a battlefield into a strategy game — one you can actually win.

6. The Trap of Emotional Reactivity

The fastest way to lose the human game is to react emotionally rather than respond intelligently.

When someone insults you, your ego wants to fight.

When sales drop, your fear wants to panic.

When money grows, your greed wants to rush.

That's when you must pause.

Observe the emotion before it becomes action.

Between *stimulus and response* lies a small space — and that's where your power lives.

Every wise leader I've met shares one habit:

They never react instantly.

They breathe, watch, and respond with clarity — not emotion.

7. The Emotion Behind Leadership

Every great leader masters one emotion — **calmness.**

Calmness is not weakness. It's controlled energy.

In leadership meetings, I've noticed something powerful—people mirror the emotion of the person they respect most.

If you're anxious, your team becomes tense.

If you're composed, they gain confidence.

That's why leadership is emotional engineering.

You design the mood in which others operate.

8. Reading People — The Silent Language

Words can lie.

But eyes, tone, and micro-expressions rarely do.

When someone says "I'm fine" but their shoulders drop—they're not fine.

When someone agrees too quickly, they might be afraid to disagree.

To master the human game, don't just listen to words — listen to the *energy* behind them.

Most communication happens without speaking.

Observe enough, and people will tell you everything without saying a word.

9. Self-Emotion Mastery: Winning the Inner Game

The hardest person to manage is not your employee or partner — it's *you.*

If you can master your own emotions, you can master almost any situation.

Here's a simple rule I live by:

"Never let your emotion speak before your mind has thought."

Train Yourself Daily:

- When angry — stay silent.
- When afraid — breathe.
- When happy — stay humble.

- When sad — reflect, don't drown.

Emotional maturity doesn't mean you don't feel — it means you *control what you express.*

10. The Emotional Formula for Success

The greatest formula I've learned in business and life:

Emotion + Awareness = Power

Emotion – Awareness = Chaos

The more aware you are of what you feel, the more power you gain.

The less aware you are, the more others control you.

Once you see emotions as signals, not masters, you start winning the human game.

You stop reacting, start responding, and make decisions that last.

11. Final Reflection

The human game is not about being smarter than others— it's about being *more aware* of yourself and them.

When you understand that people act from emotions, not logic, life becomes clearer.

You stop taking things personally.

You stop over-explaining.

You start influencing silently.

> **"Emotions run the world — but awareness runs emotions."**

That's the secret of human psychology, leadership, and money —

The game isn't out there.

It's inside you.

Chapter - 6

The Science of Connection – How to Talk So People Listen

People don't remember what you say.

They remember how you made them feel.

In business, in leadership, in life — connection is everything.

You can have the best product, the clearest strategy, the smartest plan — but if you cannot connect with people, nothing moves.

At Wakati Pharmacy, I learned this truth day by day:

Customers, employees, suppliers — every person has a story, a fear, a desire.

If you ignore it, they ignore you.

If you sec it, understand it, and speak to it — they follow you naturally.

1. People Are Listening with More Than Their Ears

Most people hear words. Few people **listen to emotions.**

When a customer complains, they don't just want a solution.

They Want:

- Validation — "I am being heard."
- Empathy — "You understand my problem."
- Respect — "You treat me seriously."

The same applies to your team. If an employee comes up with an idea, their first concern is: *"Will they value me, or dismiss me?"*

Connection begins when you realise.

Words are secondary. Emotions are primary.

2. The Power of Presence

Your presence communicates before you speak.

When I walk into my pharmacy or a meeting:

- Are my shoulders relaxed?
- Are my eyes focused?
- Is my tone calm, confident, and open?

People feel your energy first. If it's welcoming, they open up.

If it's closed or anxious, they shut down.

Presence is the silent language of trust.

3. Asking, Not Telling

Connection is built on curiosity.

Instead of telling people what to do, ask them questions:

- "What challenges are you facing?"
- "How would you approach this problem?"
- "What do you need to succeed?"

Asking shows you care.

It shifts the conversation from instruction to collaboration.

It turns employees into partners, customers into allies.

4. Mirroring: The Hidden Tool of Rapport

Human psychology loves familiarity.

People trust those who *mirror* their behaviour subtly — posture, tone, or speech rhythm.

At Wakati Pharmacy, I've used this naturally:

If a supplier speaks slowly and carefully, I slow down.

If a team member is energetic, I meet their energy.

It's not an imitation. It's *empathy in motion*.

When people feel understood, they open doors — for collaboration, for sales, for loyalty.

5. Stories Over Instructions

Humans are wired for stories, not bullet points.

A customer doesn't remember your list of benefits.

They remember the story you told about how your medicine helped someone like them.

A team member doesn't remember your command.

They remember the story of how you overcame a challenge together.

Stories engage emotion, create memory, and build connection — the foundation of influence.

6. The Listening Loop

Connection isn't one-way. It's a loop:

1. Listen actively
2. Reflect on what you heard
3. Respond thoughtfully
4. Check understanding

This loop transforms ordinary conversations into meaningful relationships.

At Wakati Pharmacy, this practice turned complaints into loyalty, questions into insight, and conversations into action.

7. Language That Resonates

Words matter — but *how* you say them matters more.

Use simple language. Avoid jargon.

Speak clearly. Pause. Emphasise the most important idea.

Most importantly, align your words with your values.

People sense authenticity. They reject hollow statements immediately.

"Connection is 20% words, 80% alignment between intent and expression."

8. Emotional Anchoring

People remember moments, not messages.

Anchor your key ideas to emotion:

- **Gratitude:** "I appreciate your effort; it matters to me."
- **Curiosity:** "I wonder how we can solve this together?"

- **Vision:** "Imagine where we can be if we do this well."

Emotional anchors stay longer in memory than facts. They make people feel part of something bigger.

9. Connection Is Leadership

Every great leader I've studied and every experience I've lived shows the same truth:

- Employees follow leaders who connect
- Customers stay loyal to businesses that connect
- Partners invest in people who connect

Connection is not optional. It's the **currency of influence**.

It is how trust grows, teams thrive, and businesses scale.

10. Closing Reflection

Connection is a science and an art. It requires awareness, empathy, and practice. It requires listening more than talking, feeling more than instructing, and leading with heart more than ego.

> "You can have the best idea, product, or plan — but if you cannot connect, it remains invisible.
>
> Master connection, and you master influence."

At the heart of every human relationship — in business, in leadership, in life — is one question: **Do I feel seen, heard, and understood?**

If your answer is yes, you follow. If not, you walk away.

Master this, and you master the human game.

Chapter - 7

The Psychology of Money – Why Wealth Starts in the Mind

Most people think money is about numbers.

It's not. Money is about beliefs, habits, and emotions.

The richest people in the world aren't always the smartest.

They are the ones who understand how money works inside the human mind.

In my journey with Wakati Pharmacy, I discovered early that financial success is more mental than material.

How you think about money determines how you earn, spend, invest, and grow.

1. Money Is Emotional Energy

Money is a tool, but it carries emotion everywhere it goes.

People fear losing it, crave it, justify it, or fight over it.

Even in business, I've seen this:

- Employees hoard resources because they feel insecure
- Customers hesitate to pay because they feel mistrust
- Suppliers demand upfront because they fear being cheated

Your first step in mastering money is understanding that **all decisions are emotional first, logical second**.

Money isn't neutral — your beliefs about it shape reality.

2. The Scarcity Mindset vs. Abundance Mindset

I grew up poor, working in a small shop carrying rice bags and sugar.

At that time, every rupee felt scarce. I learned to value it. But scarcity also teaches fear.

Scarcity Mindset Says:

"I can't afford it. I might lose. I'll never have enough."

Abundance mindset says:

"There's opportunity. I can grow. I can invest and create more."

At Wakati Pharmacy, I had to constantly switch from scarcity to abundance.

Investing in licenses, training, or supplies felt risky at first—but thinking abundance helped me grow my business instead of staying stuck.

3. Money Reflects Your Beliefs

Ask yourself: "What do I truly believe about money?"

- Do you think it's evil? You'll resist earning it.

- Do you think it's only for the lucky? You'll avoid risk.
- Do you think it's a tool to create impact? You'll use it wisely.

Your inner belief about money becomes your financial reality.

This is why wealthy people often share the same mental patterns: they **take money as an opportunity, not security**.

4. Discipline Over Desire

One of the hardest lessons in business is managing desire.

When Wakati Pharmacy started earning, I faced a choice:

- Spend every rupee for comfort and status
- Save, invest, and reinvest for growth

Desire is emotional; discipline is mental.

Emotions push you to spend, fear pushes you to hoard, but discipline builds wealth.

The psychology of money is simple:

Control your mind first. Money will follow.

5. Risk and Reward Are Mental Games

All investments are psychological.

Risk scares people. It also excites them.

At Wakati Pharmacy, I learned to analyse every opportunity:

- What's the upside?
- What's the downside?
- Can I recover if it fails?

Most people avoid risk because of fear — not because the math is bad.

Mastering fear is the real secret behind all calculated risk-taking.

6. Financial Freedom Is a Mindset

Wealth is not just accumulation.

It's freedom. Freedom from stress, from dependency, and from fear.

I realised early that financial freedom starts in the mind:

- Budgeting with clarity
- Investing with intention

- Spending consciously

Money is a reflection of mental clarity.

Confused thoughts = unstable finances.

Clear strategy = predictable growth.

7. Money Follows Value

The human brain is wired to exchange value for value.

You cannot earn money without creating something someone else wants, needs, or trusts.

At Wakati Pharmacy:

- Customers paid because they trusted the service
- Employees worked hard because they believed in the mission
- Suppliers partnered because the system was fair and reliable

Money flows naturally when you create value, build trust, and serve consistently.

8. The Compounding Effect

Wealth is like a snowball — it grows slowly at first, then accelerates.

The psychology behind it is patience, consistency, and trust in the process.

Saving small amounts, reinvesting profits, nurturing relationships — all seem insignificant early.

But over time, they compound — not just financially, but mentally.

This is why long-term thinkers always outperform short-term thinkers in life and business.

9. Lessons from My Journey

Here are the core money lessons I've learned through experience:

1. Money is emotional first, logical second.
2. Shift from scarcity to abundance mindset.
3. Discipline beats desire.
4. Fear is the biggest barrier — master it.
5. Create value first; money will follow.
6. Financial freedom starts in the mind, not the bank.
7. Patience compounds results faster than urgency.

10. Closing Reflection

The real secret of wealth is not more work.

It's **mental mastery** — understanding fear, desire, risk, and value.

If you master your psychology, your money will master itself.

And that is how true financial freedom begins.

> "Money doesn't make you rich. Your mind does.
>
> Money is just the reflection of your thoughts, beliefs, and actions."

Chapter - 8

Building a Business That People Love

A business is more than products, profits, or processes.

It's a living system made of **people, trust, and energy**.

From my years building Wakati Pharmacy, I learned a simple truth:

"A business grows fastest when people love it — employees, customers, and partners alike."

Love is not a soft word. It is strategic.

When people feel cared for, understood, and respected, they **work harder, buy more, and stay loyal**.

That's the invisible engine behind every sustainable business.

1. Start With People, Not Products

Many entrepreneurs focus on products or profits first.

They forget that people — customers and employees — are the heart of business.

At Wakati Pharmacy, our first rule was:

"Serve people first, money second."

This Mindset Shaped Everything:

- Employees who feel valued stay and grow
- Customers who feel respected return and refer
- Suppliers who feel trusted deliver on time and on better terms

Business isn't about transactions. It's about **relationships**.

2. Build a Culture, Not Just a Company

Culture is the invisible framework that guides behaviour.

It's what your team does when no one is watching.

At Wakati Pharmacy, I focused on building a culture of:

- Respect and transparency
- Accountability and ownership
- Learning and curiosity
- Empathy and collaboration

Culture turns ordinary employees into passionate ambassadors.

It turns ordinary customers into loyal fans.

3. Service Is the Foundation

People remember experiences, not products.

A pharmacy can sell the same medicine as any other store, but what makes people choose Wakati is **how they are treated**.

Simple practices make a difference:

- Greeting customers warmly
- Listening to their problems
- Following up with care
- Being honest when a product is unavailable

Service is the bridge between psychology and business.

When you serve genuinely, people feel it — and they reward it with loyalty.

4. Lead With Vision, Not Fear

Fear-driven management may get results in the short term, but it kills long-term growth.

I've Always Led Wakati Pharmacy with Vision:

- A clear direction for the business
- A mission employees can believe in
- Goals customers can trust

When your team sees a future worth building, they don't just follow — they **create it**.

5. Systems Multiply Success

People alone cannot scale a business; systems ensure consistency and quality.

At Wakati, We Developed Clear Systems For:

- Inventory management
- Sales and marketing
- Customer relationship management
- Employee training and incentives

Systems don't replace people; they **amplify their effort**, reduce stress, and ensure everyone can perform at their best.

6. Money as a Tool, Not the Goal

Profit is the reward of value creation, not the purpose of business.

In my early years, I reinvested every profit back into Wakati:

- Expanding inventory
- Training staff
- Improving customer experience

When money is a tool to serve people, growth happens naturally.

When money is the goal, trust and loyalty vanish quickly.

7. Feedback Loops Are Gold

Business is a conversation, not a lecture.

Feedback from customers, employees, and partners is priceless:

- Listen actively
- Adapt quickly
- Implement changes thoughtfully

At Wakati, every complaint became an opportunity to improve.

Every suggestion became a chance to innovate.

The businesses people love are always **learning businesses**.

8. Emotional Intelligence in Every Decision

Every decision — hiring, investing, marketing — should account for human behaviour.

- How will employees feel?
- How will customers perceive it?

- What's the long-term impact on trust and culture?

When emotional intelligence guides your strategy, people feel valued, respected, and motivated — and they naturally love your business.

9. Storytelling and Identity

People connect to stories, not brands.

Wakati Pharmacy is not just a pharmacy. It's a story of hard work, perseverance, learning, and trust.

Communicate Your Story Consistently:

- Why the business exists
- Who it serves
- What it stands for

When people identify with your story, they don't just buy from you — they believe in you.

10. Closing Reflection

Building a business that people love is not a formula.

It's A Philosophy, A Practice, And A Mindset:

- Lead with empathy
- Serve with passion
- Build with integrity

- Reinvest in people, not just products

A business that people love becomes unstoppable. It grows quietly, sustainably, and beautifully — like Wakati Pharmacy has.

> "Businesses don't fail because of markets.
>
> They fail because they forget people. Put people first, and money, growth, and success will follow naturally."

Chapter - 9

Scaling Without Losing Your Soul– How to Grow and Keep Culture Intact

Growth is exciting. Growth is necessary.

But growth is also dangerous.

Many businesses expand rapidly and then collapse — not because the product failed, but because the **culture, trust, and values** that built them were ignored.

Scaling is more than opening new branches, hiring more staff, or increasing revenue.

It's about replicating what works without losing the soul of your business.

1. Know Your Core Values

Before you scale, you must be crystal clear about **why your business exists and what it stands for.**

At Wakati Pharmacy, we defined our core values early:

- Trust above all
- Service before profit
- Empathy in every action
- Continuous learning

These values became the **north star**. Every decision — from hiring to expansion — was filtered through them.

Without core values, growth becomes chaos.

2. Systems Are the Backbone of Scale

People can work hard, but human effort alone cannot sustain growth.

Systems ensure consistency, efficiency, and quality as you grow .

At Wakati Pharmacy, We Developed Systems For:

- Sales tracking
- Customer relationship management
- Inventory and supplier management
- Employee training and performance evaluation

When systems are aligned with values, your culture travels with the business.

Without systems, even the best team collapses under pressure.

3. Hire for Culture, Train for Skill

When expanding, the temptation is to hire the most experienced people quickly.

But skills can be taught. **Culture cannot.**

Every new hire at Wakati Pharmacy had to align with our core values.

We invested in training and mentorship for skills, but **attitude and alignment came first**.

This principle protects your culture even as your team grows.

4. Empower Leaders Within

You cannot scale alone. You must create leaders who reflect your energy and values.

I trained team members to take ownership of processes, resolve conflicts, and inspire others.

Leadership energy doesn't weaken when shared — it multiplies.

Scaling without losing soul requires leaders who carry your culture as a living force.

5. Standardize Without Sterilizing

Scaling often requires standardisation: same procedures, same quality, same experience.

But beware — over-standardisation kills creativity and warmth.

At Wakati Pharmacy, we standardised service quality but allowed personal connection to flourish:

- Customers were greeted by name
- Staff could solve small problems their way

- Flexibility remained within the structure

This balance keeps growth consistent without losing the human touch.

6. Maintain Customer Connection

As your business grows, it's easy to get lost in numbers.

The real test of scale is **how customers feel**.

Even at multiple locations, Wakati Pharmacy maintained:

- Personal follow-ups
- Listening to feedback
- Addressing complaints quickly

Scaling is successful when **every customer still feels important**, not just another transaction.

7. Financial Discipline in Growth

Expansion is expensive. Rapid growth can drain cash and stress operations.

I followed a simple rule:

"Reinvest profits first, take calculated risks second, never compromise the core business for short-term growth."

Scaling sustainably is a financial strategy as much as a psychological one.

It requires patience, planning, and emotional control.

8. Protect Your Team Energy

A growing team can create friction, stress, and burnout.

Leaders must actively protect the energy of their people:

- Regular communication
- Recognition and appreciation
- Conflict resolution
- Opportunities for learning and growth

A team that feels supported will carry the culture forward, no matter how large the business becomes.

9. Iterate, Don't Copy Blindly

Every new market, location, or opportunity is slightly different.

Copying your existing model blindly is a recipe for failure.

At Wakati Pharmacy, Each Expansion Involved:

- Studying customer behaviour
- Observing local culture
- Adjusting systems without changing values

Scaling without soul is about **adaptation, not replication.**

10. Closing Reflection

Growth is a test of discipline, values, and emotional intelligence.

Your soul is your business's compass.

If you lose it, money, systems, and customers may follow, but your business will eventually crumble.

Protect your culture. Train leaders. Standardise wisely. Serve with heart.

When you scale this way, **your business grows in size and in love, trust, and impact** — just like Wakati Pharmacy has.

> "Scaling is easy. Scaling with integrity is hard. Scaling with integrity and culture is rare."

Chapter - 10

Building a Legacy – How to Make Your Business and Leadership Last Beyond You

Every entrepreneur dreams of success. Few think about **lasting impact**.

A legacy is not measured by money in the bank or number of branches.

It is measured by the **values, culture, and influence** you leave behind — the ripple effect that continues long after you step away.

From my journey with Wakati Pharmacy, I've learned that building a legacy is intentional. It requires vision, discipline, and the courage to think beyond the present.

1. Define What Legacy Means to You

Legacy Starts with Clarity:

- Do you want to leave wealth, wisdom, or both?
- Do you want to leave a culture of integrity, innovation, and trust?
- Do you want your business to serve communities long after you are gone?

For me, Wakati Pharmacy's legacy is about **trust, service, and empowerment**.

Money alone cannot define a legacy; influence and impact do.

2. Embed Values in Every Layer

A business survives when values outlast founders.

At Wakati Pharmacy, I ensured:

- Core principles were part of the training and systems
- Leaders and employees understood *why* we do what we do
- Decisions were always aligned with purpose, not just profit

When values become a habit, they persist even when leadership changes.

3. Empower the Next Generation

Legacy is built by growing leaders, not followers.

I Mentor My Team To:

- Take ownership
- Lead with empathy
- Solve problems creatively
- Uphold company culture

A business survives if the next generation carries the vision forward.

A leader who does not empower successors leaves a business that may exist, but not thrive.

4. Document Systems and Knowledge

Knowledge dies when it exists only in your mind.

At Wakati Pharmacy, we documented:

- Operational systems
- Customer management practices
- Financial strategies
- Leadership principles

This ensures that your methods, wisdom, and strategies are preserved.

Legacy is easier to sustain when **systems carry your vision**.

5. Create Impact Beyond Business

A legacy extends beyond profits.

I Focus On:

- Building trust in communities
- Supporting local healthcare
- Training young professionals

- Giving back through education and mentorship

When your business contributes to society, it becomes **part of a larger story**, not just a transaction-based entity.

6. Lead With Purpose, Not Ego

Ego-driven leadership is short-lived.

Legacy-driven leadership is intentional, humble, and consistent.

Every decision I make for Wakati Pharmacy asks:

"Will this strengthen the culture and values long-term?"

"Will this help people beyond immediate gain?"

Legacy is about **impact over recognition**, about planting seeds you may never personally see grow.

7. Cultivate Emotional Intelligence in Your Successors

A business can survive systems but flourish only through **emotional intelligence**.

I ensure leaders and team members are trained to:

- Understand and manage their emotions
- Build genuine connections
- Lead teams with energy, empathy, and clarity

A business that feels alive to people will last far longer than one that is purely transactional.

8. Measure Success Differently

Legacy is measured not by quarterly profit, but by:

- Cultural strength
- Loyalty of customers and employees
- Influence on the community
- Systems that sustain performance

Wealth, expansion, and awards are secondary. True legacy is a **sustainable positive impact**.

9. Teach Others What You Know

Knowledge without sharing dies. Legacy is **educational and replicable**.

I write, mentor, and train — not just for Wakati Pharmacy, but for future entrepreneurs who will carry forward the lessons I learned.

The real value of your work multiplies when others can apply it in their own lives.

10. Closing Reflection

Building a legacy is the ultimate act of leadership and purpose.

Wakati Pharmacy is more than a business.

It is a story of perseverance, discipline, trust, and human connection.

It is proof that if you lead with purpose, nurture culture, and master both people and money, your impact can last far beyond your lifetime.

> **"A business that serves people, a team that thrives, a culture that lasts — this is the real wealth.**
>
> **A legacy is not what you leave behind for yourself, but what you leave behind for the world."**

Epilogue

Your Journey, Your Blueprint & Key Takeaways

Integration of Lessons:

- People first, money follows
- Emotional intelligence and presence matter
- Values and culture guide sustainable growth
- Legacy is impact beyond self

Key Takeaways:

1. Relationships drive success.
2. Money is a mental game.
3. Leadership energy multiplies influence.
4. Connection and empathy are the foundation of trust.
5. Culture preserves soul during scaling.

6. Serve first, profit follows.

7. Continuous learning is non-negotiable.

> "Work hard, learn deeply, lead with heart, and build a legacy bigger than yourself."

Key Takeaways:

1. People Are the Heart of Every Business

- Relationships with customers, employees, and partners matter more than products or profits.
- Listen, empathise, and serve genuinely — people buy trust, not just goods.

2. Emotions Drive Decisions

- People act on feelings, not logic.
- Learn to read emotions — yours and others' — and influence decisions wisely.

3. Leadership is Energy

- Lead with calmness, presence, and integrity.
- Your energy sets the tone for your team.
- Empower leaders to multiply your vision.

4. Connection is Influence

- People remember how you made them feel.
- Ask more than you tell.
- Use storytelling, mirroring, and active listening to build trust.

5. Money is Mental

- Wealth starts in the mind — beliefs, habits, and mindset matter more than numbers.
- Shift from scarcity to abundance.
- Reinvest profits wisely, manage risk, and create value consistently.

6. Culture Is Your Compass

- Values guide decisions, especially in growth.
- Hire for alignment, train for skill.

- Systems protect and amplify culture during expansion.

7. Scaling Without Losing Soul

- Standardise processes, not empathy.
- Maintain customer and employee connection.
- Adapt to local context without compromising core values.

8. Legacy Is Your True Measure

- Legacy is not wealth — it is lasting impact, culture, and influence.
- Mentor, document systems, and train leaders.
- Build a business and life that continue to serve others long after you are gone.

9. Continuous Learning is Non-Negotiable

- Read, observe, and reflect.
- Every challenge is a lesson, every failure a teacher.
- Emotional intelligence, financial literacy, and leadership skills are lifelong pursuits.

10. Serve First, Profit Follows

- When you focus on creating value and serving people, money, growth, and success follow naturally.

Final Words

Building a business, mastering money, understanding human psychology, and leading people are not separate skills — they are **parts of one integrated journey**.

Your mindset shapes your money.

Your energy shapes your team.

Your empathy shapes your customers.

Your culture shapes your legacy.

If you take these lessons, apply them consistently, and stay true to your values, you will not just succeed — you will create a business and a life that **people love, respect, and remember**.

> "Work hard, learn deeply, lead with heart, and build a legacy bigger than yourself."

Chapter Summaries & Action Steps

Chapter - 1

My journey – From Village to Vision

Summary:

- Overcame early life challenges and poverty.
- Learned the value of hard work, discipline, and perseverance.
- Early jobs taught systems, teamwork, and resilience.

Action Steps:

1. Reflect on your personal story — what lessons can guide your business?

2. Identify the skills you learned through adversity.

3. Use your past experiences as fuel for growth, not limitation.

Chapter - 2

The Mind Before the Money

Summary:

- Mindset shapes success. The difference between winning and losing is how you think, not what you have.

- Emotions drive decisions. Fear, desire, ego, and validation control more choices than logic ever will.

- Scarcity is mental. Wealth begins when you stop focusing on what's missing and start creating.

Action Steps:

- Pause before decisions — ask, "Am I acting from fear or clarity?"

- Reframe money beliefs — replace "I can't" with "I'm learning how."

- Read people, not just numbers.
- Start your day calmly — silence builds clarity, clarity builds power.

Chapter - 3

The Psychology of Trust

Summary:

- Trust is the foundation of business, sales, and leadership.
- People buy, follow, and invest in those they trust.
- Trust grows through consistency, empathy, and integrity.

Action Steps:

1. Identify key relationships in business and evaluate trust levels.
2. Commit to one action daily that builds trust.
3. Always align words with actions — check for inconsistencies.

Chapter - 4
Leadership Energy

Leadership is energy in motion.

It is not about a title or position. It is about:

- **Presence** — how your energy affects others
- **Focus** — clarity in decision-making
- **Empowerment** — multiplying your influence through others

A leader's energy sets the tone. Calm, confident energy motivates; anxious, inconsistent energy demotivates.

Action Steps:

1. Observe your energy daily and its effect on others.
2. Mentor at least one person this week.

Practice calmness under pressure.

Chapter - 5

The Human Game

Summary:

- Emotions drive decisions more than logic.
- Understanding human behaviour is the key to influence.
- Emotional intelligence empowers leadership and communication.

Action Steps:

1. Observe one emotional reaction each day and reflect before responding.
2. Identify five emotional drivers for key stakeholders.
3. Practice pausing before acting on strong emotions.

Chapter - 6

The Science of Connection

Summary:

- People remember how you make them feel, not what you say.
- Connection is built through presence, empathy, and active listening.
- Stories, curiosity, and emotional anchoring strengthen bonds.

Action Steps:

1. Practice listening more than speaking in every conversation today.
2. Tell one story that connects with your team or customers this week.
3. Notice how your presence influences the energy in meetings.

Chapter - 7

The Psychology of Money

Summary:

- Money is emotional; wealth begins in the mind.
- Scarcity vs. abundance mindset shapes financial behavior.
- Discipline, value creation, and patience compound success.

Action Steps:

1. Reflect on your beliefs about money — are they limiting or empowering?
2. Track income, expenses, and savings for one month consciously.
3. Identify one area to invest or reinvest for growth this quarter.

Chapter - 8

Building a Business People Love

Summary:

- Success comes from relationships, trust, and value creation.
- Culture, service, and emotional intelligence drive loyalty.
- Vision and consistent service create long-term business love.

Action Steps:

1. Evaluate your business culture — what is working, what needs improvement?
2. Identify three ways to improve customer experience immediately.
3. Share your vision clearly with your team this month.

Chapter - 9

Scaling Without Losing Your Soul

Summary:

- Growth must preserve culture, values, and trust.
- Systems, leadership empowerment, and adaptability are key.
- Standardize processes but maintain flexibility and empathy.

Action Steps:

1. Document one critical process to ensure consistency.
2. Identify potential risks to culture in upcoming growth plans.
3. Train a team member to lead in alignment with your values.

Chapter - 10
Building a Legacy

Summary:

- Legacy is impact, culture, and influence beyond yourself.
- Empower successors, document systems, and mentor continuously.
- Lead with purpose, not ego, and measure success by influence, not wealth.

Action Steps:

1. Write down your legacy vision — how do you want to be remembered?
2. Identify at least one future leader to mentor intentionally.
3. Implement one initiative that benefits the community or team beyond profit.

Epilogue

Integrating Lessons into Life and Business

Summary:

- Success integrates people, psychology, leadership, and money.
- Values, emotional intelligence, and culture are non-negotiable.
- Apply lessons consistently, and your business and life will thrive sustainably.

Action Steps:

1. Create a daily reflection habit — review decisions and energy.
2. Choose one lesson from each chapter to focus on this month.
3. Commit to continuous learning — read, observe, and refine practices consistently.

Acknowledgements

This book is a piece of my heart — built from the lessons, love, and guidance I've received from so many people in my life.

First, I dedicate my deepest gratitude to **my father, Jaswant Ram**, and **my mother, Geri** — my first teachers, who taught me the true meaning of hard work, simplicity, and faith. Every value I hold today began with them.

To **my mentor, Ankur Warikoo**, author of *Do Epic Shit*, for inspiring me to think deeply, act bravely, and create with purpose.

To **Mr. Bhanwer Patel**, my manager at Toyota, who guided me with wisdom and showed me how leadership truly works.

And to **my friend, Ravi Mathur**, who became the bridge to my life's biggest change — the journey to Africa, to Tanzania.

To my brothers — **Anop and Sunil**, and my sister **Guddy**—who I grew up with, learned from, and laughed with.

Anop, who now stands beside me as the **Managing Director of Wakati Pharmacy**, is not just my brother but my closest friend and strongest support.

I don't just have siblings; I have life companions who have been with me in every step of this journey.

To **Mr. Hetul** from *Medox Pharma*, who was truly my *MBA of life* — teaching me how business really works, not from books, but through real experience and daily discipline.

To **Mr. Gopal and Mr. Punit**, for believing in me and trusting me to start *Wakati Pharmacy*. Your faith became my foundation.

To My Entire Family —

My wife, **Himanshi**, my Bhabhi **Chandana**, my brother **Anop's wife Mamta**, and the little ones, **Pari, Golu, Dala, and Dhibhali.** I love you deeply. You all have a huge share in making me who I am today.

To **my Wakati Pharmacy team** — from Hira, Mr Manager, our delivery heroes, our sales and store teams—thank you. You have stood with me through every challenge.

We are not just a team; we are a family with a shared dream. Believe in yourself — you are far more than a team; you are the soul of Wakati.

And to all **my friends around the world**, I may not name everyone here — because that would take another whole book — but know that I am grateful for each of you.

From our laughs, arguments, and lessons — I've learned something from all of you.

Special mention to **Samar Ahmed**, **Gyanji**, **Tarang, Dilip** and my village buddy — your friendship still lives in my heart.

To everyone who believed in me when I was just beginning — this book is also yours.